Seduction

PassionPoet
Robert R Gibson

Copyright © 2023 Robert R. Gibson

All rights reserved.

ISBN: 978-976-96544-2-6

No part of this publication is to be copied, transmitted, or recorded in any form, except for small snippets for the purpose of review, without the prior, express, written permission of the author.

An

Erotic Empire

Book

Editing / Book Layout by
Passionate Words Editing Services

(IG @passionate.words.editing246)

Dedication

Seduce me,
Lyrically…
Let your words slip into me
Rhythmically
Until I am quite moist –
Literally.
Speak to me in whispers
Till my yoni breathes
Consistently with
You as oxygen.

This book is dedicated to all the beautiful people who are turned on by mental stimulation, by the intellectual intercourse of sensual words slowly stroking your mind until your body responds. This book is for you…

Acknowledgements

I want to acknowledge Lisa Lipps, Ainsley Carter and Empress Poetry for their valuable additions to this volume of work – I enjoy each poet individually and having them together in this book makes me happy.

I also want to acknowledge every single person impacted by my words. You are the reason why I enjoy what I do. As I always say - my wordplay is my foreplay, and you give me a reason to continue writing!

Table of Contents

Prologue — 13

Part 1 Seduction & Culmination — 15

    Preamble — 17

    I Want To Fuck A Poet — 19

    Poet Speaks — 23

    Seduce Me — 25

    Double Penetration — 27

    Ménage à Trois — 29

    Disintegrate — 33

    Urge — 35

    Listening — 36

    Surprise — 38

    Honey Jam — 40

    Self Discovery — 42

    Revealed — 44

    Shy Goddess — 46

    Roleplayin' — 48

    Let Me Be Your Toy — 51

    Come — 52

    Work Of Art — 54

A Satisfied Bottom	55
Turbocharged!	59
Hunger	62
Fantasy	64
Fetish	66
Sweet Treat	68
Out to Lunch	70
I Don't Want to Fuck...	72
Make Love To Me	74
Give In To Me….	76

Part 2. Afterglow — 79

Afterglow (Gogyohka)	81
Marriage (Gogyohka)	82
Morning Ritual	83
The Journey	85
Exquisite Beauty	88
This BlackMan Smiles	90
Empress	91
Heat	92
Sleep's Puzzle	94
Star Light Wish	95
Kundalini	96

Infinity	98
Offering	100
Lost	101
Permission	102
When	104
Dedication	105
Pursuit	107
You Are My Reflection	110
Perfect	111
Soul Mate	113
Silver's Song	114
The Pledge	116
Epilogue	*118*
About the Author	*119*

Introduction

Seduction has been aptly defined as 'Enticing the mind to gain access to the body', and this second anthology does just that.

The poems within this collection are designed to reach deep into your consciousness, make you **FEEL** intensely and make your whole body react in bliss…

Open the pages. Start the **SEDUCTION**.

…and remember:

ROBERT R. GIBSON, THE SENSUAL WORD ARTIST KNOWN AS **PASSIONPOET,** IS NOT TO BE HELD LIABLE FOR ANY POPULATION EXPLOSION IN ANY PART OF THE WORLD WHERE THIS BOOK IS READ!

Prologue
Venus Rising

Playful
Joyful
Life abounds
And brown eyes twinkle

"Come, play with me…"

Seductive winks
Caramel skin ripples
Nipples harden
And Passion
Stiffens…

Locs fly free…
She smiles,
And I melt into
a pool of liquid
Desire…

Pleasure's invitation
Pink petals open
Passion's insertion
Arousal heightens
And
Waters flow….

Baptising
Worshipping
Foaming

At the Temple of Venus,

I kneel ….

And Venus rises.

Part 1
Seduction &
Culmination

Seduction

Preamble

My goddess glistens in the moonlight
Breasts upright, begging me to reach...
Skin slides on skin as oil warms
And I stroke, fingers seeking heartbeat.
Love shines in your eyes as we link stares
And I cup breasts in hand
Feeling their weight, loving their curves.
Fingers are feathers and touch is gossamer;
Under touch's spell, nipples take note -
and rise...
As eyes fall into the eternity between seconds,
Lips follow suit, and touch....
And the earth stops in that instant.
Lips slowly trickle down
Form cups around left nipple
as I increase suck-tion, I feel ripples of desire
And I wonder if I inspire such in return...
I suck and tongue, feel nipples pebble
as fingers travel towards your promised land
Seeking liquid answer to my riddle
Digit slipped slowly into slit
Finding clit awake and ready
With ambrosia dripping steady from exposed cleft.

aaaaaahhhhhhhhhhh!

She wants me too!

Fingers linger at your centre

Seduction

Before plunging boldly onwards,
I enter you with two fingers deep
and slowly call out your explosion
with a steady come-hither motion
Bucking hips start their rotation
Gasping breath stifle orgiastic moan
And I am bathed in oil, how my skin shone
in the moonlight! Your release is sweet!
I remove fingers and suck off your joy
And rub the droplets into my skin
As I begin again at opened cleft
This time with tongue!

~~~

Let me drink from fountain of youth;
Hips rock in rhythm as tongue invades sacred space
And ambrosia flood flows down anxious sluice gate.
All praises to the Goddess as she releases!
I kneel in reverence, face toward sacred tabernacle
And bow, ingesting holy water from Goddess' chalice.
I lap at the rim in rhythm with moaning hymns
And plunge tongue deep within to the very dregs.
Spread legs my arches, feminine petals my portal
And I am transported to ever higher planes of enlightenment.
"Gush my Goddess," your humble servant cries,
"I am yours to command, yes, yours to enjoy…"
As ecstatic trembles take over your temple
I continue the ritual of Holy Communion
Taking the Sacred victuals - I eat and drink
And in response, my nature rises
My chakras open and I am willing to serve….

Seduction

I Want To Fuck A Poet

PassionPoet:

I want to fuck a poet

I want to suck stanzas
from your skin
Lick lyrics from lips
parted in desire
And taste tangy tankas
when I go down on you.
We might even write
a new haiku...

Coz

I want to fuck a poet

I want to feel
the beat as
Head meets breast
Rhythms ripple
from erect nipples
While tongue dances
Finding the perfect cadence
as it teases
And pleases

I want to fuck a poet

Seduction

I want you
To spit spoken word
On my mic
So our night
Would be full of
Rhythm and flow:
We rock in rhythm
Until sonnets flow
from swaying hips
Then flip the script
As you flip your slit
Presenting your assonance
And I enter you from behind
Penetrating you with
My rigid rhymes...

I want to fuck a poet

I want onomatopoeic orgasms
Want ooohs and aaahs
And uh
uh
uh
A climax that's coming
coming
Climbing the scales in octaves
So strong that the waves
Become hyperbolic
Exaggerated sonics
That can be heard
For miles around…

Seduction

Coz, see…

I want to fuck a poet!

Lisa Lipps:

I want to fuck a poet

I want his beautiful mouth to claim my nipples
Making me speak stanzas in a language only known to lovers.
I want the rhythms of his verses to make my body
Dance to the song only he can sing.

I want to fuck a poet

I want his stanzas to stand strong as he enters my lines
Demanding me to match his words with my expressions.
I want to explore the
Iambic pentameter of his God given rhythms
Matching my cadence to his
As we spiral ourselves into
Haikus of complete satisfaction.

I want to fuck a poet

Create limericks that can only be spoken
By the sounds our bodies make
As we entwine ourselves into moist pleasures
only imagined by the greatest lovers of all times.

I want to fuck a poet

Seduction

Perform rhythmic verses that flow from my centre
Drowning you in lines that satisfy your guilty pleasures.
I want to feel the thunderous climax to your story...
Leaving us satiated and limp in each other's arms.

Yes... yesssss... yessssssss...
That is why....

I want to fuck a poet....

Seduction

Poet Speaks

Tongue stroking phallic words majestically,
Making climax auditory
As words rise and fall with the rhythm of lovers
Rising and falling together…
Rising
Rising
Rising together
Falling
Falling
Falling forever…
Into bliss…
Tumbling around
Rumbling
The sound of the poet as
He tickles the nether regions of your mind
Places kinda … intimate
Making you get into his groove
As his stiff vocals tease and move
into you in one smooth….
Thrust-
ing into your mind
resigned to
Give in to the feelings
Overwhelming all reason
'tis the season for pleasure,
Exciting adventure
Searching to find
The treasure hidden

Seduction

Within the folds of skin ...
In your ear....
His words excite
Causing mood to spin
Out of control
Impossible to get a hold
Of yourself
Shivering with intensity...
Words designed to blow your mind
Make you wet
Get you stimulated to
the brink of oblivion....

The poet speaks
Words draw to a close
Leaving you naked
Exposed
And not even care
As you swear you can feel his hand cup your sex
Oh baby ...
Oh baby...
Yes, yes, yes, right there...

And as he breathes his final line
You feel the climax come

One
Final
Time....

Seduction

Seduce Me

Seduce me,
Lyrically…
Let your words slip into me
Rhythmically
Until I am quite moist -
Literally.
Speak to me in whispers
Till my yoni breathes
Consistently with
You as oxygen.

Fill me with the fullness
Not just of your penis
But bring to me the edge
And hold
Me
There
As we teeter on the climax
Of stimulating conversation…
So good that
I just
Can't
Stop!

So….
Make love to me
Mentally
Before you ever touch my body

Seduction

Let me crave the
Need of you
Inside my
Mental cavity
Stroke my cortex
Liberally
Until your poetry
Makes me moan
And until we
Can't help ourselves
And have to join
Physically

'Coz being apart any longer
Would surely be
Torture…

So, please….

Seduce me,
Lyrically…
Let your words slip into me
Rhythmically
Until I am quite moist -
Literally.
Speak to me in whispers
Till my yoni breathes
Consistently with
You as oxygen.

Seduction

Double Penetration

I pierce your mind.
Stiff syllables slide slowly –
Rhythmically –
Between cranial folds,
Injecting ideas deep into intellect
Making cerebral cortex spin
Into
Intimacy's infinitesimal vortex.
Poetic turns of phrase turn you out
As I slip inside you over
And over
And over again
Making mind cream with desire…
Making mine spurt intellectually
Impregnating your thoughts
With the seed of our combined consciousness.
As conversations connect us
To the core,
Are you coming to your own conclusions
after our conscious discourse?
After prolonged intellectual intercourse
That made inspiration scribble Braille across our skin
And made us both spill thoughts onto virgin sheets
As proof of our consummation...

Which made us hunger?

I pierce your flesh.
Intelligence the ultimate aphrodisiac,

Seduction

Making natures rise;
Craving to cum inside
From the cold.
Spurning separate space,
Clinging desperately to same air;
Sampling breath shared by Passion's longing
To taste desire on parted lips
Undulating hips
Sample nectar from weeping slit.
Slipping me into you
Realising we fit
Together
Perfectly
And we ride the waves of bliss,
Feeling seduction's kiss,
Not desiring to miss the opportunity to become one
Bodies go where minds have forged the trail
Merging joyously with abandon
Claiming the right to conquer
Which was already offered...
Rocking bodies finally succumb to pleasure
Immeasurably overcome by overwhelming sensation
Uniquely caused by double penetration.

Seduction

Ménage à Trois

My heart stirs as you open wide
Your mind excites me
Don't hide your thoughts
Your words make me stiffen
In anticipation of entering your secret place
Don't worry - I'll set the pace
With rhymes and rhythms
To make you squeal
My lyrical love makes you wet
And sends us both to the edge of reason
This is the season to be alluring
My heart speaks, and during my oration
I pour a libation
Inviting you to consummate
our conversation... R.G

I suckle on your libations
For your metaphors and haikus speak volumes of unwritten
prose to my hungry soul
Sensuality oozes from my pores while my hips dip low to
accompany your load
Feed me till I want no more
My heart and heavens spread wide in anticipation
I anticipate total annihilation
Of this plethora of emotions you have stirred
I am besotted by your spoken word
This is indeed the season for our passion to be heard
And during your dictation, a chorus of elation
Escapes my lips......E.P

Seduction

Words to soothe
given birth to poetic
lyricists
displaying affection
and eroticism
as I suck on your body
like a cannulae
filtering your blood
throughout your body
As it keeps us perked and erect
.......you collapse
experiencing a lyrical orgasm....A.C

Your cries move from sensual sighs
To guttural moans
As my pen is honed on the sharpness of your wit
I enter you
Mind hit with every lyric
My pen's prowess used to impress
This lyrical Empress
My words fail to express
How much my mind is blown
By lyrical lips fastened to me
orally, you tickle my fancy
My ears get hot
Gimme all you got
Talk your talk
You're hitting my spot.. R.G

I move from the page to the stage
Eager to rock your mic

Seduction

Salivate my thoughts like droplets of dynamite
Ready to explode while you implode
Inside of me
My cup overflowing
Ecstasy from knowing, I'm hitting your spot
Just one word from you and I go from simmering to hot
Instantly, come on King, enter me
Your wordplay, is like foreplay
I'm ready for the main course.......E.P

Would you eat or be eaten as your body calls
You think you can handle me?
Only one way to find out
Cheap thrills
As the lyrics spills
exploding in phenomenal cries of ecstasy
She thought she could lay motionless
But under the flickering of my tongue
Her body became one
As I played musical notes with every thrust
Up and down... A.C

This feels so right it can't be wrong
Temperatures rising higher with every round
I'm going down for seconds
This has to be the best, I reckon
At least for me
Stuck in between erotica & sensuality
Receiving this penetration lyrically
I'm begging you to plant that word in me
So I may give birth to POETRY.... E.P

Seduction

Copywritten © 2012 by

Empress Poetry

(http://www.facebook.com/EmpressPoetry)

Robert Gibson

(http://www.facebook.com/BajanPassionPoet)

Ainsley Carter

(http://www.facebook.com/mrxqwsit)

Seduction

Disintegrate

Fingers sinking slowly
Seeking shape of orgasm
curling around my desire
in a 'come hither' motion
I want you
to come to me

Come….
Cum for me
Yesssssss

I….
Watch you moan as I stroke your walls
Legs spread
Finger buried deep within your treasure
Seeking bliss of hidden pleasure
Going ever deeper
Searching for the source
of ecstatic river
Flowing onto questing member…
And I keep stroking
Eyes locked in mutual rapture
I spell out my need
My greed to feel all of you apparent
One finger is not enough -
I have to enter another;
So slowly extract me from you
And taste glistening heaven…

Seduction

mmmmmmmmmmm

Before two digits
Reintroduced to slit
and slip again past pearly gate
By slowly tweaking fleshy knob
I release your flood
Slide inside your wetness
Fingers doing little to stem the tide
Emotions collide as crescendo builds
And builds
And builds
And builds
Until
You disintegrate…

Seduction

Urge

Seductive stares lock, earth stands still;
Nature holds breath as
Sizzling tongues spark molten heat
Desire shaped hickeys branded on
Heaving breast
Arms lock
Bodies rock
Searing insatiable fury of plunging kisses
Neck flung back, rapture rises
Skin bared in flurry of *Now*
Stepping over the line
No turning back
Drink the ambrosia of the gods
Cupped to catch the downpour
The storm breaks
Electric emotions break past reason's dam
Tension snaps
Release it all!
Fast and furious, thunderous squall
Plunging into depths of awakened passion
Clung skin to skin
Sweat to sweat
Engorged entrance ecstatic to be filled
Oil slick, pleasure spilled
Enormous tremors rock our worlds
Lovers curl
And Earth exhales.

Seduction

Listening

I always listen
To my inner
Goddess
When I'm
In her
Goodness…
I listen when
I hear her
Moan my name
An unending
Refrain
Of passion
Audible reaction
To the insertion
Of my will –
Unbreakable
Commanding respect!
I hear no objection
As prosecution rests
And I pass sentence,
As bodies tense
Then relax
Under waves of whimpers.
Her body whispers
And I listen
Listen to hear her
Resonate with pleasure
As I finger her
Treasure,

Seduction

As I measure
The levels
Of her desire…

I always listen
To my inner Goddess
When I'm in her...
And I hear her
Perfectly!

Seduction

Surprise

Eyes closed
Mind wondering
Candles burning
Body yearning
for your love…

Heart fluttering
Music playing
Juices flowing
Petals dripping wet
Wait …
He hasn't touched me yet….

Fingers clenching sheet
Foreplay on repeat
Bodies meet and greet
Legs open
Words unspoken

shhhhhhhhhhh

Fingers on lips
As he glides
between my hips

Deep penetration
with stiff erection
Hours of steamy affection

Seduction

Bodies moving
in sensual motion
Under the spell
Of your magic potion

Ecstasy…
Put it on me!

Body numb
Explosion…
I've just cum!

Seduction

Honey Jam

Filled with honey
As I saw you smile
Thick and sweet and runny
My desire is molasses
Dark
Wanting to trickle over you like treacle
Wanting to taste you
Jam myself into
The centre of
Your pleasure
And eat the sweet treat
Arousal secretes
I want to couple
With your supple mind …
I find
I can't sleep –
Breath gasping,
Desire rasping –
Pumping heart,
Steady thumping drum
Beating out my fiery thoughts:
Empress! Goddess!
Envelop me in slick
Divinity
Let matching thrusts
Mirror carnal lust …
To know you intimately –
Not just physically,
But meld mentally

Seduction

Bodies held together
By the closest tether…
Sweetest nether honey —
Thick and sweet and runny.

Seduction

Self Discovery

I wish I could take you in my arms
And kiss you
Just once
And in that kiss would be all my desire
All the fire bottled up in me
That I can't release easily
Want to pull you close and caress your face
Trace the path of tears down your cheek
Seek to expunge you of the pain
You try not to reveal
And conceal behind a smile
When all the while your heart is breaking
I want to plunge inside you
Skin to skin
Breaking a sweat
Whetting your appetite
Making you crave more
Like an addict needing another hit
Another fix
As we six-
ty nine
And knot into sublime
Sexual configurations
Not just because you draw me
In
Like moth drawn to fiery grave
But because I want to
Paint self-assurance on your skin
Confidence in your curves

Seduction

Give birth to
A sense of worth
Because seeing you excites me
Our conversations thrill and
Delight me
And self-doubt is a blight, see
Robbing you internally
From seeing the full extent
Of your beauty
Not just emotionally
But physically
So know, my love,
That really
There is more to you than you realize
And what I see with my eyes
Makes me want to explore
Learn more
And be a part of your
Self-discovery.

Seduction
Revealed

Lisa

Lazy breezes move the curtains as I relax across our bed.
Fresh from the shower, I've chosen Victoria's Secret in peach.
I hear your footsteps but choose not to react.

Sprawled on my belly with only my panties on, I feel hands
on my back and realize you now have a plan for me.
Grabbing my orange oil from the nightstand, you stream it
onto my skin and begin to massage my body.

The strength of your hands arouses my hidden pearl as I
breathe in the mingled scents of your body, sun warmed
winds and citrus.
I try to remain prone and enjoy your touch but my growing
desires betray me.

Rolling onto my back, I see the burgeoning bulge of your
manhood and immediately my floodgates open.
Feminine pheromones and oranges mingle with the breeze as
a wet spot forms at the meeting of my thighs and you....
Become entranced...

Your only desire is to have my treasure
Revealed.

Passion

Hand over mound, intense desire pours through my palms,
Making your centre flood with the need to be filled.
I claim your wetness – massaging your nub rhythmically;

Seduction

Hips rock in tandem to my questing digits
And the scent of wanton heat mingles with orange massage oil
Making me delirious.

I want you. Now.

Fingers grip fabric, forcing moans from needy lips
I silence you with hungry tongue down vibrating throat
Heart beating, breaths increasing.
Eyes locked, naked desire consuming
Feeling your hips writhing,
Hips moving in soundless screams:
"Fuck me…."

Manhood stiff, needing release
I let cloth fall, showing rod in all his glory
Yet, one more barrier needs to go…
And, with practiced slowness,
I pull peach panties away from sopping slit
Wanting nothing more than to have your treasure
Revealed.

Seduction

Shy Goddess

Why so shy, Goddess?
Coz I…
I am already impressed…
You in repose like a
Regal Empress
My eyes drink your beauty
Like a thirsty man trudging the Sahara.
Go on… let me see…
Drop your arms, let your breasts free
To be caressed by my gaze,
Lovingly tracing nipples until they pebble;
Till gasps come in spasms
And shivers trickle down spine
As I suckle your skin, as though fine wine
Bursts spontaneously from each pore.
What's more … your ink excites me…
Makes me want to carefully trace each pic with my tongue,
Trying to taste the stories each one has spun
While getting to know you
Inside and out.
Finger tracing your hips
And slipping seductively into weeping slit
As tongue travels slowly down to meet it,
Becoming intimately acquainted with stomach dip –
Navel – for the uninitiated.

Why so shy, Goddess?
Parted legs show forth your flower
Scent arouses, seeking to overpower

Seduction

Reason …
'tis the season to be devoured
And not to be timid
Your creamy skin makes me stiff and rigid
Getting ready to enter
Exploring the depths of pleasure's centre
But it has to wait its turn…
I have already started to churn inside
With finger and tongue on clit
Legs spread wide
As I enjoy you.
Your taste – Ah! Ambrosia of the Gods
Drips down chin as I keep plundering
To seek the last of divine nectar
Leaves me wondering if I could die
Just
Like
This
And be immediately transported
To eternal bliss
So that I could pleasure you
Infinitely
Rod slowly invades your intimacy
And we
Melt into each other
Completely

So … I ask again…

Why so shy, Goddess?

Seduction

Roleplayin'

Black panty
Entices me
Winks cheekily as you
Lay before me
All chocolatey
Not just your skin
But the sweetened syrup
You are pouring
All over breasts
Left me staring
And
Salivating

Without waiting
I suckle

Lick cool chocolate
Off alert nipple
Suck until ripples
Of pleasure travel
From swelling peaks
To between the cheeks
Of your ass

You wiggle
Enticing me with
Your sexy giggle
And I invade your navel
With my tongue

Seduction

Swirling around and around
Excavating the indenting
In your belly
Removing the cherry
You left for me

Fingers kneading;
I continue feeding.

Following the chocolate trail
I lick and suck and kiss your skin
And pause as I am nearing
Your centre
Removing silky barrier
I enter you
Tasting the pudding
Made by chocolate syrup
And female yearning

Stirring your desires
My tongue enquires after your taste
Dipping in again to
Satisfy curiosity
No longer a mystery
Your pussy calls to me
And I answer willingly
Tickling the fantasy
We have laid out carefully
Beforehand

Your hips rotate
Feeling muscles undulate

Seduction

Under my attention
Causing a little distraction
But your satisfaction
Is within my grasp
Hearing you gasp
As I clasp your knees
And pull them wider
I'll let my tongue
Be the saddle
You are the rider

I replace my tongue
With a buzzing bullet
Slip it into your pussy
And full it
With vibration
I feel you resonate
With the connection
We feel together
Your moans alone
Make me harder
But I will not succumb
To temptation
Tonight is about you
And as you squirt your
Liquid elation
- Get the wet wipes! -
And
We rejoice in the affirmation
That our role-play
Started out this way….

Seduction

Let Me Be Your Toy

Hey baby
Come here…
No, don't be afraid…
There's nothing to fear
Don't stare in fright at
My apparent frown
Just put that piece of plastic down!
That's not what you need.
It may give you temporary reprieve,
But can you conceive
The pleasure you will derive
From sitting astride this noble steed?
You may wonder if a mechanical hum
Is the only thing that will make you cum

But

I want to strum your cervix like an African drum
Calling the ancestors with our combined rhythm
Stroke deep and long, leaving you breathless and numb
From the real deal
(Your) Rod of Steel
Yet soft enough to be your first meal of the day….
So, what do you say….
Just put that plastic thing away
And let me be your Toy today….

Seduction

Come

You bid me come … and I do.
I fall into your big beautiful eyes
And long to feel the
smoothness of your skin under
probing fingers.

I feel the fire of my Passion rising
as I plunge my tongue deep
into the recesses of your mouth
And taste your desire as we kiss.

I will not miss this chance.

One glance at your beauty and all control is lost;
I must come to you at any cost -
Hands gripping as I start climbing twin peaks
Letting flesh speak as I tweak their summits.
They pebble under my attention
Resistance plummets – and I keep falling
I hear your need calling –
You start to moan as tongue goes lower
Teasing apart each petal on your flower
Seeking sweetness of hidden nectar

And …

And as it starts to flow
I know I've found my ambrosia
For you … you taste heavenly

Seduction

And I'd climb Mt Olympus daily
To sample your sugar eternally

But now … now, I'm ready…
I enter you oh so slowly

With bodies kissing in bliss of heated touch
Skin on skin, we rock to the rhythm of us
Intimacy, started slowly increases friction's frequency
Until synapses fire, screaming for release
And we climax together, simultaneously

You've bid me cum

And

we do.

Seduction

Work Of Art

Let me paint your yoni with my tongue,
Mixing kaleidoscopic sensations
upon the palette of your skin,
Making your body writhe in artistic poses
as I skillfully wield my brush;
And, as much as you might beg me to stop,
I cannot interrupt my flow -
Your taste is my muse, I'm an erotic Picasso
That burns to capture your essence
In the multi-coloured hues
of multiple orgasms.
My brush dips,
Slips sweetly across your canvas;
Etching my Passion into your flesh
with goosebumps.
Let me paint you into a work of art,
Chipping away at resolve with every stroke,
Carving out a masterpiece of
mutual manifestations of bliss,
Transferring the glimmer of anticipation
To actuality's solid form.
Bringing inspiration's vision birthed in my loins to fruition
And, as my brush strokes quicken
I intend to capture the intensity
of our awakened kundalini
And splash explosions of colour
upon the coital composition
That is us.

Seduction

A Satisfied Bottom

"I've been bad…"

Eyes downcast.
Shame darkens air
Sunny smile hidden
Behind angry rain clouds.

No words necessary -
Not now…
Spilled like sugar crystals
Sparkling on the counter-top
Wasted.

Useless.

Just like before;
You were spoken to - sternly,
Yet you repeat offence…
Just recompense your only reward.

"Come."
You know what's next
Try to recoil
Reversing.
Conversing - trying to
Bargain out of punishment
But I'm not having it…

Sitting on the straight backed chair

Seduction

Shroud of silence hangs
Tears trickle down your face
You stare like a deer in headlights
Rigid

One step
Two steps
Three.

You stand before me
Bend at the waist
Lay prone on my lap
Waiting.

Skirt raising
Voice shrill
"NO! Not bare!"
Panty ripped down
Uncaring.

Spanks torrential downpour
Soak skin in seconds
Pain leaks from eyes
As you struggle to be silent
Finally obedient.

Then dam breaks.
Sobs spill through cracks in resolve
And with it, anger evaporates.
Replaced with desire

Slaps slow

Seduction

right
down
To
Sensual
rubs

Tears give way to
Moans
As fingers slip
Softly
Out of sight
And emerge
Glistening.

Spank and slide
New game we play
No longer punishing
But pleasuring

And I slick my fingers
On your clit
Slit slick with want
As my other hand
Spanks your left ass cheek
Just so…

You grind your pussy
Upon my hand
No longer caring
About sparing dignity
I spear you again
While taking liberties

Seduction

With probing fingers

And the clit
I make it jump
And pulse
The sting of the slap
Vibrating towards needy nub
Again
And again
And again

Till pants flood with joy
as you release
but I'm still rubbing out
your resistance
on the hardness
of your clit.

Seduction
Turbocharged!

No...

We don't always have to go slow
I want to take you with quickness
Show you I'm able to handle this...
Want to throw you down
Spread petals wide
Slide inside with the speed of a NASCAR driver
Take you higher and higher
Till oxygen levels lower
And you have to gasp for air...
Or is it for pleasure?
I want to stroke deep
Strong
Long
Until my rhythm makes you weak
And until every word I speak
Makes liquid seep
From the hidden place where thighs meet
And where my lips pick
Orgasms like orchids.

No...

We don't always have to go slow...
Let your mind go
And let us crash into each other
With urgency
Let the frequency of our joining

Seduction

Increase exponentially
Over the square root
Of our lust's
Consistency.
There's a time and place
For sweetly seductive sensuality
But – this is not it.
Let's make sweat drip as we
Wrestle for dominance
As I try to flip you on your back
As I work to make
You
Cry
Out

I wanna hear your scream my name
Bite my neck
Be driven insane by
The power of the shiver
As you came
And stayed
And went
And …
And…
And…

Ummmm….
What day is it again?

Left is right
Up is down
The space time continuum

Seduction

Has ruptured…

Damn….

So …

Drivers –
Start your engines!

Let's not go slow…

Seduction

Hunger

Eyes close

Fingers slip slowly

Down dampened skin

Wandering

Tracing my heat

Need overwhelms

I must release

I grip my breast

Bite my lip

Legs part like River Nile

While fingers seek

Vainly

For dry land

Seduction

Hand dips into moist intensity

Fiercely finding fleshy knob

I turn the faucet

And start to flow

I stroke out my desire

Trying to cool my heat

Extinguish the fire

Focused between my thighs

I scream out my release

And rest

Until buildup starts anew

And I have to renew

My fingers' search

To feed my hunger…

Seduction

Fantasy

Let me be your
fantasy
All wrapped up
in mystery
Hidden identity
intrigues me
makes me forget
the harshness of
reality
that overpowers me…

But here...

Here I can be master
you can be slave -
no, not slave -
be my muse
Amuse me as we play
Inspire me to write
sonnets on your skin
And as I slip in-
side you
We consummate our in-
timacy
We fulfil our fantasy
and then we

switch roles
change masks

Seduction

and do it all over again!

Seduction
Fetish

You might think me fresh – maybe crazy

But can you give me a peek?
Want to see your panties –
That sight stirs up my fantasies;
Blue, or white or pink … something lacy
Cut in a boy short or barely
There thong…
I can't go wrong…
The voyeur in me stirs whenever I see a flash of skin
A raised skirt, legs parted invitingly
Makes me go back to school:
Schoolboy clumsily drops a pencil
While he fumbles
Looks up and stumbles
The sight of heaven makes control crumble
Strip of pink winks back at him
And he's hooked like a fish being reeled in…

Now, back to the present.

I want to slip my gaze under your skirt
For quick peeks, let my eyes flirt
With your pussy -
Satisfying my raging curiosity.
Want to know what you are wearing
Under that skirt – so short, it's daring!
Want to see your panties slipping
From hips to floor

Seduction

Exposing more and more of the treasure
Hidden under that lacy pleasure….

I want to kneel before your centre
Feeling wonder as I prepare to enter
With my tongue
I slip your panties down
And inhale deeply in meditation
Arousal's incense raises excitation
Passion's expectation
Is to blow your roof off with penetration
Want to ruffle your poised presentation
Of composure
Facilitating more exposure
So come, my beauty, let us start
Part those lovely legs
Let me see
The colour of your lacy panty…

Seduction

Sweet Treat

Cream, whipped
Spread on slit
With aplomb

Parted legs my dish
Fulfilling your wish
Your
fantasy

To be
My
dessert…

Topped with cherry
Ready …
To be popped

Fruits rained down…
yoni sprinkled
with
strawberries and
pineapples
winking in the light
peeking through
the
sweetest topping

of
chocolate

Seduction

syrup

Ready
to be
slurped

lips licked
as I
sit

Enjoying the view

My sensual meal
not yet complete

My banana swells
ready to split
you
open

After I eat…

Seduction

Out to Lunch

I just want to share my thoughts with you.
Can I?
I'm thinking…
You would look delicious spread out for me to sample
Like a delectable buffet of desire dancing on my palette
I'm thinking…
Tasting you would be an experience
Akin to drawing in the deep essence of a ruby red wine
And feeling it dance with joy as flavor copulates with tongue
Effervescently
So I can truly become one
With you…
I'm thinking …
I wouldn't want to miss juicy thoughts as I take your pearl
And swirl slowly
Sucking seductively
Like
I'm thinking that
I don't want to miss the honey
That be
Dripping down to my waiting lips
As I sit at the table
And dine
I'm thinking…
I'll be slipping effortlessly between your folds
As I unfold you
Successfully combining lusty fervour with
Gentlemanly behaviour.
I'm thinking…

Seduction

Being intimately introduced
To your Southern beauty
Orally
Is fucking fantastic.
I'm thinking…
I'm sinking deeper into my meal
As I hear you moan and squeal out your pleasure
I measure out the portions I allow myself…
I can't over-eat…
Gluttony is still a sin, right?
I'm thinking…
I'm thinking…
I'm thinking…
I'm thinking it's time for me to start cooking
So that we both can enjoy our meal
When I start eating!

Seduction

I Don't Want to Fuck...

I don't want to fuck...
I want to caress your cerebral cortex with my cadence
Till your labia drip with my words;
Want to make your aura shake with my verbal essence.
I want to speak oracles with my tongue,
Sliding seductively over skin in sentences slipping in and out of you with conviction.
I want to palm your breasts with the power of my phrases;
Want to encircle nipples over and over and over again
With the tickling sensation of a good stimulating conversation,
Bringing them to a standing ovation at the cessation of my oration.
I don't want to fuck….
I want to pull panties down as we pontificate,
Wanting to engage your hips in healthy debate
Where opposing arguments go back and forth in heated discourse,
Rolling vigorously under our persuasions, each one trying to get the upper hand,
Beads of sweat breaking out like bullet points accentuating each thrust.
I don't want to fuck.
I want to create climactic conclusions after our vigorous tête-à-tête
And then, while you're still wet, whisper that I have one more point to make,
And will penetrate quickly to consummate the ultimate connection.

Seduction

You see – I don't want to just fuck….
I want to make love.

Seduction

Make Love To Me

Come: make love to me.
Want to feel your kiss plumb
Deeply into my soul…
So passionately
it makes knees weak,
tongue numb can't speak,
breath spent; shiver went like lightning
to lowest point AND highest peak
short circuiting every nerve ending
seeking release…
no peace for the aroused…
wanna hold you close
Till hearts intertwine …
Till I am yours
And you are mine with
Genuine intimacy…
Until we find the ultimate connection –
We merge until our two becomes, on
Closer inspection, one complete whole:
Unique parts give multi-faceted reflection
As we cum together, completing orgiastic injection.
Wanna feel your skin, with feather touch
Say it all without much words
Every action heard while rising …
writhing between the junction of your thighs
with sighs of contentment as we fit
flat head's bit to screw's small slit…
then turn…
body yearns for more - screw tightened –

Seduction

tensions heighten; motions increase
titan effort to keep total control....
Relax... unroll ... and kiss...
Small actions releasing pent up bliss;
That send liquid heat right up my spine
As we recline upon each other's desire
As we inspire each other to rise
To the occasion
Orgasmic sensation sought diligently
Like explorers scanning eagerly
For the exact spot excitedly marked
'total ecstasy'....
Come, make love to me....

Seduction

Give In To Me....

"Give in to me…"
Eyes lock. So much said without a word being uttered;
Scriptures recited in seconds as my lust burns behind my stare.
Slowly I reach out, tracing side of face with fingers extended —

And, we kiss. Temperatures rise; 0 to boiling in three seconds flat…
Match lit, thrown on the dry kindling of unattended attraction,
Desires blazing in an inferno of need that cannot, will not be extinguished!
My body calls, "Give in to me…."
Tongues twirl, seductively swirling in ever swelling arcs,
Hands crush bodies possessively, instinctively trying to share same space.
Kisses move from your face, to the curve of your neck;
Sliding palms traverse spine, resting, then gripping the curving flesh.
Skirt slides up, slip of fabric slides down
And flesh on flesh I knead your cheeks.
My body calls, "Give in to me…."
Tongue traces breast, nipples harden
Breath is caught, all senses sharpen…
Top is discarded…
Breast exposed, then covered with heated attention
Sucks and licks ensue with passionate intention
Legs spread of their own volition, and, unbidden,
Liquid need starts to moisten your apex.

Vortex of emotion circles around your centre
Following the path of questing, exploratory finger
That dips once, twice, inside your wet entrance....
And you melt.
My body calls, "Give in to me…."
My stiffness meets your wetness
Slipping hardness into softness…
Rhythmic prowess snarls powerfully
As I take your terrain for my conquest!
I lay claim to this land, each thrust driving flagpole into earth
And shrieks of pleasure raise as I plunder your treasure
You cum with a flourish, as though I was signing my name,
And with a kiss you turn over; we start all over again…
"Give in to me…"

Part 2.
Afterglow

Seduction

Seduction

Afterglow (Gogyohka[1])

Sweet silence sings
after climactic crescendo
nestled intimacies…
lullabies…
peace…

---

[1] **Gogyohka**: a five-line poem developed by Enta Kusakabe in Japan that translates literally to "five-line poem." It's a derivative of tanka that uses natural phrasing to great effect.

Writer's Digest: "Gogyoka: Poetic Forms" - https://www.writersdigest.com/write-better-poetry/gogyohka-poetic-form

Marriage (Gogyohka)

Two doves encircle
One heart
Two souls intertwine
One life
Together

Seduction

Morning Ritual

My desire lights a fire
under my pen
Inspires a verse
to spring unhindered
From my thoughts
A carefree deer
Bounding from word
To word
Skipping happily
Through syllables
Climbing rocky pinnacles
To the climactic summit.
Thinking of you lets verses
Fly free
The most beautiful poetry
Flows from my heart and goes
Straight home to roost on yours
A homing pigeon with
My latest love letter
Strapped to its leg.
I think of you and words dance
On the page
Cavorting on the stage of
Our attraction
My words vie for your attention
One smile from you
Is an honourable mention
And I collect my prize
Staring at your eyes

Seduction

And sharing passion
With a fiery kiss.
Thoughts become words
Expressed as verse
Until pages are filled
And my heart is stilled
Until the next thought comes
And stirs my heart anew
To start the cycle again…

Seduction

The Journey

want to kiss my way from
toes to fingertips
making the trip
s…l…o…w…l…y
taking in all the sights along the way
noticing the little scar on your knee
from the day you fell out of the breadfruit tree
and tracing the rough edges of the place
where mosquito bit – leaving a trace
of her love bite

and I do the same,
soothing with a kiss.

silky thigh makes me sigh with
softness of tender skin
wandering,
my tongue has thoughts of plundering…

I pull it back into line
and continue my journey
tracing each curving hip
with heated breath from questing lip
I pass over the rolling hills of your behind
remembering the first time
I saw your birthmark

I have no haste while
arms encircle willing waist

Seduction

not wanting to miss anything,
I stop to take in the view -
how breath taking!

You

are exquisite, so divine
I start again the meandering climb
carefully scaling sloping spine

with kisses.

Tongue plays connect the dots
drawing lines between each freckle

but not to draw a picture

I'm seeking all your pleasure spots
Gently parting flowing locks
I make my mark on nape of neck,
teeth carving, "I love you," into tender bark

Kissing slowly down shoulder blade
noting carefully the goosebumps made
as trailing fingers trace your back
lips close to journey's end

I suck each finger – turn over
now
for the trip back

Seduction

d
o
w
n
.
.
.

Seduction

Exquisite Beauty

You are not cute.
You are exquisitely delicate
Like fine expensive china.
Your beauty sparkles off
Your smile like the light
Twinkling on diamonds,
Hitting the right
Angle as you
Turn towards me
With the face of an
Angel.
I am awed by your beauty
Want to hold you close to me
And kiss you
Tasting the sweet nectar
Of your essence.
Having the closeness of your presence
Melt into me….
You are not cute.
Your beauty is rarer than the jewels
Honed from the dusky soil
Of similarity
All others dull with mediocrity
As I marvel at the
Incomparability
Of your smile.
Even the midday sun
Pales in deference
Dims in significance

Seduction

And shies away in reverence
As I see you radiate
Your essence
When you come near.
You are not cute.
Your beauty stops me in my tracks –
My breath is halted
I forget to breathe
As I marvel in the wonder
That is you…
Your voice plays softly with my ears
Whispering away and soothing fears
That you might leave again…
And although I know you
Are rarer than the most expensive
Gem
I know for certain
That you are *not* cute.

Seduction

This Black Man Smiles

This black man smiles.
Bathed by the light of the twinkle in your eyes
Washed by the liquid joy flowing from lips
Drawn back in a grin as our eyes meet.

This black man smiles.
Sensual curves tempt hands, wrapping around waist
Pulling toward me in erotic embrace
Tempting lips to touch in electrifying connection.

This black man smiles.
Regal presence shatters heart's defences
Empress crown cascading down supple back
Makes me shiver as I drink in your essence.

This black man smiles.
Arms linked together, hearts synced doubly strong
Minds joined inseparable .

This black man smiles
Thinking about you.

Seduction

Empress

Beautiful Black queen, regal Empress,
Your words inspire me, makes me want to impress
You, express the way my stomach flip-flops around you;
Your words make me shiver, I have to suppress
My voice's quiver, without success
As your presence overwhelms me!
Listening to your flow makes me go weak in the knees –
I've never had a feeling like this!

You stand tall, beautiful and proud;
Shapely: lovingly crafted by the Master Sculptor…
I dream of unleashing the lioness within
Releasing your wraps, wrapping my heart within your locs
Like a garment, writing my feelings on my soul like
parchment…
Drinking in the essence of royalty
Your hands encircling mine transfer power, spoils me
For the touch of your energy
And no one else can consume me completely
By just a word, a glance, overwhelmingly
Sensual, yet carrying this amazing beauty
That stops me from speaking
As my heart seeks your eyes – meeting
An Empress in the flesh.

Seduction

Heat

Flash fire blazes with
stoked liquid heat
Stroked rhythmic beat
evokes
faster expressions
of desire's connections
As passion ignites
setting bush alight
with stick's frenzied friction
against pleasure's lighter fluid
Rising heat forces shedding sheets
Sweating skin
Burning lips
Churning hips
Yearning within
To be filled to the brim ....
With you
Flash fire love blazes high and quick
Reason's smokescreen dark and thick
Emotions' dry kindling catches easily
Consuming all reasoning completely
Till nothing remains
But regret's ashes

****

Heat starts slow
Fire fed with care
Dedication
Fanning with

Seduction

Concentration
Needing to last
Can't let it die
Must continue to burn
Food to prepare
Hearts to keep warm
Lives linked to share
Forever transformed
Love's passionate flames
Controlled
Focused to a beam
White hot blowtorch love
Not to be messed with
Dangerous if handled incorrectly
But, used in right hands,
Deftly used to fuse
solder smouldering souls
Into one synchronised life -
Husband and wife -
Inseparable.

Seduction

Sleep's Puzzle

Arms pull you close
Drawing living essence
From your presence
As chin finds comfortable seat
In the crease between
Your neck and shoulder,
Nose pressed to skin
Drinking you in
Back pressed to chest,
Best protection against cold air
Snuggling deep into lover's embrace
Slowly stroking lock of hair
Rebelliously tickling naked cheek
Sneaking from behind the ear
Like little girl playing hide-and-seek
Joined at the hip, we slip
Into a comfortable place
Two pieces fit together
Love's jigsaw puzzle
Now complete.

Seduction

Star Light Wish

Star light Star bright / First Star I see tonight
I wish I may, I wish I might / Have the wish I wish tonight…

I wish …. for you…
Your soft lips caressing mine,
Soft touch begging for another
And another and another and…
falling from the precipice of reason
Into maddening desire…
Probing tongues duelling, hands pressing skin to skin
Hearts pulsating with passionate salsa rhythm
As sweat glistens off gleaming mind yearning
For the touch of heart to heart – of emotions churning
Away at the raw core of our souls…
I wish for you….
I long to plumb the depths of your inner core…
Make you sing my praises as you come
To the brink of imploding sensations
And then recede again
Away from the shore
Deceptively retreating
Tide building under the surface
Till tsunami's crescendo overwhelms
Overpowering rushing ….
And until you lay in my loving arms …. spent.

Seduction

Kundalini

I
Bow to the light in you
Suckle at the breast
Feeding my spirit with
Your essence
Building
My inner man
With your glory.

My
Fingers stroke your
Yoni in reverence
Dipping past flower's
Petals to
Touch heaven.

I
Enter your
sacred space –
Honoured to share this
Holy moment with
You

Joined by
Tongue
Fingers
Lingam

Energy moves

Seduction

As bodies do
And yet, not…

For we two
Shall not share
Same space
Until deemed ready
Until Universe
Deems it so

So we
Will join on planes
Astral and
Virtual

Yet no less
Real

Show me
Your sacred space
Again

Let me bask
In your
Light.

Seduction

Infinity

I am
Plugged in
To
You

We two
Form one
Circuit

We fit.

As

Yoni
Joins
Lingam

Electricity
Surges
with
Carnal urges

Kundalini
Rises

Creativity
Copulates

Impregnates

Seduction

Full term gestation
Releases
Hidden potential

Elemental embryo
Now birthed
As fully formed
Idea

We two
Form one
Circuit

We fit

And slip
Into the eternal
As ideas are birthed
And released
To form new
Ideas
Of their own.

Seduction

Offering

I seek to enter the Sacred space:
The place of birth,
Of gestation;
My adoration is palpable – physical – sacrificial …
So I do not come empty handed.
I bring everything I am to the house of worship –
The place where Goddess dwells,
Where seeds swell with limitless potential –
And I offer everything willingly.
Take everything I have to give
Everything I am
And
As I enter your Holy of Holies
Slowly
As I worship …
with
Rhythm and thrust
And as the Spirit leads us
I release all my seed
And then lay still
Praying for the increase.

Seduction

Lost

There is nothing new under the Sun
everything has already been sung or put to verse
but that doesn't stop my heart from singing your praises
doesn't stop my soul from penning rhymes
in awe of your smile, your laugh
the feel of your body against mine
the way your eyes sparkle with joy
the thrill of your swaying hips on the dance floor
wanting to run my hands through your locs……
No, there is nothing new under the sun
but indulge me as I repeat myself
and lose myself
in thinking of you…..

Seduction

Permission

May I tell you
How much I love you?
May I count the days
Until we touch?
May I dream of
Hand holding
Laughing
Kissing
Knowing
That you and I were
Meant to be
Eternally....
May I hold
My heart on
My sleeve
And open
Up my
Soul so
You could enter
Me?
May I burn
With a fire
Only you can cool?
Or would you
Instead be my
Incendiary device
So when friction
Causes heat
We explode?

Seduction

May I love you
Like you need to be -
Fiercely
Intensely
Completely
Consuming
Until nothing remains …
May I?

Seduction

When

When I first saw you, the earth stood still
My heart paused in the eternity between seconds
My breath stopped, I couldn't breathe
And then you spoke
My faculties returned with a vengeance
As I heard you say my name
When we first kissed, passion ignited an inferno in my heart
Flames of desire shot out, engulfing reason
Burning all rational thought to cinders
My lips touched yours and my emotions erupted,
Instructed my hands to move across your body
Exploring each nook and crevice…
When we first made love our connection was intense
My heart in suspense
As our bodies moved in sync with our inflamed desires
Building slowly from rhythmic dance to orgasmic crescendo
….
And when I lost you…
My heart rent in two
The pain of my loss overwhelmed me completely
Grey thunderstorm and pelting rain
Hid my tears as I slowly watched
You leave.

Seduction

Dedication

I dedicate this piece
To the most beautiful woman in the world.
This piece sings her praises
Like a choir of angels sings around the Throne of Grace
This piece swears loyalty
Like a defendant swears to tell
The truth, the whole truth and nothing but…
The truth is, this piece is totally smitten
It is the poem to end all love poems.
It is the beginning and has no ending
Because this piece swears it believes
In reincarnation -
This piece will be reborn after this age
And will still be head over heels in love with you.
This piece is dedicated to you
Like a newborn baby is dedicated to God at birth
Dedicated to defend your honour
Like a gallant knight charging into battle
With his lady's favour tied in a knot
Above his elbow.
This piece is willing to suffer ridicule
For its unwavering devotion
Like a zealous disciple who is convinced
That he has found the way, the truth, and the light
And no one can convince him otherwise.
This piece is dedicated to the most beautiful girl in the world.
Dedicated to the one who makes this piece go silent
whenever she smiles.
Dedicated to the one whose courage rivals that of the

Seduction

Spartans
Dedicated to the one who is the sun, and this piece is the earth,
Caught in the gravitational pull of love.
This piece, and all others after it
Is dedicated to you.

Seduction

Pursuit

Forest holds
breath.
Her eyes
whisper,
"Come…."
She
ran
I
pursued
Deep into forest
Desire giving speed
to beating heart
Feet sure on
hidden path
Longing
Inspired chase
seeking
fleeting nymph
sparkling
Winking like
babbling brook,
blinking cheekily
in the sun.
Caught her
on the shore
flashing eyes
liquid fire
water crashing
fluid desire

Seduction

Wanting to hold
her
possess
her
Be one.
Natural beauty
stuns me into
Stillness.
We kissed
The bliss of our lips
slipping past
our reserve
conserved
tongues
exploring
Wrapped in
blanket of leaves
connecting with
Earth
passion exploding
Being one
resting
on
cresting
waves
emotions
undulating
under writhing vines
shivering spines
rocking in and out
of mottled sunlight
playing peekaboo:

Seduction

dark, then light
then dark again.
Our cries
joined
like our hips.
Nature
rejoiced.

Seduction

You Are My Reflection

Staring deeply into my soul through your eyes,
I see ripples of our connection in our reflection.
Your pupils dilate as we consummate our love in our gaze.
I'm amazed – no words need be said, but we're joined as
Surely as if we'd kissed and fallen headfirst into bed …
It's true! I see me in you…
And no – for once, I'm not speaking erotically,
But we're connected cosmically,
As though you and me were truly meant to be;
From age to age, from forever to eternity.
I stand at the precipice staring off into the wonder
Of the beauty of your love. I ponder what did I do to deserve this?
I can see what I need to in you – ways to improve
You inspire me to move – to not be stagnant
And just one smile drops a pebble into my soul
That ripples throughout in waves of significance
You are significant
Just the little things you do….
I look into your eyes and see myself
You are my reflection.

Seduction

Perfect

You're so ….
Perfect
In every way.
Your beauty reflects
from your eyes:
mirrors of the soul that
is perfectly aligned
with mine…

You're so …
Perfect
I sit back – amazed –
That you and I fit;
Like I am the key
That unlocks your secrets
I lock myself inside you
And explore.

You're so …
Perfect
I feel at peace
As though you are
My nirvana
And to achieve enlightenment
All I have to do
Is hold you
And meditate.

You're so …

Seduction

Perfect
Perfectly natural
What you see is what you get
And what I see
Mesmerises me and
Leaves me
Breathless

Coz you're so
Perfectly perfect
For me….

Seduction

Soul Mate

Soul mates
Souls mate
Two souls
Inseparably
Linked
Joined by love
Now found…

****

Soul mates
Souls mate
Unbreakable bond
Connected
Over distance….

****

Soul mate
Souls mate
Cavorting, linking, melting…
Two hearts merging – one heartbeat
Doubly strong.

Seduction

Silver's Song

What would I say?
I would say that...
Your voice melts my heart
Like butter left on a hot stove
Liquefied love replaces my blood
And courses through my arteries
Taking your essence to every cell
Nourishing my spirit with your smile.
I would say that your smile
Heats me up to boiling point
And the sun has to find shade
When you come out in your glory....
And when you look at me
My attention is caught like a moth
To burning flame.
Inflamed with Desire, this Passionate Lover
Sees the reason for his existence..
I would say that I would take your hand
And lead you into pleasures as we meet
Mind to mind
As our souls connect with deep conversation
And as we reveal secrets
Vulnerability is sooo sexy...
And I peel away my insecurity
To stand naked and vulnerable before you
A lion with a heart of gold.
And I would say
I've done enough talking
Time for me to listen

Seduction

Sing your Silver song around my soul
  And let us marinate together.

The Pledge

My Queen, here I stand
heart in hand, representing
me presenting my greatest gift
to you – loyalty
strong and true
more potent than any magic potion
fervent love and ardent devotion
Desire so deep it scares me
I mean, really…

I love you from your head to your toes
hair follicles to nail cuticles
and everything in between

love the strength that blazes from your eyes
passion that liquefies – dripping eager drops
down parted inner thighs
your sighs bring me to the highs and lows of rapture
you've captured my heart, now hold it prisoner

but this is a life sentence I'll gladly serve
I'm not looking to be an escaped convict
Coz I'm firm and strong in my convict-ions
that I have chosen the right one – set restrictions
on my sight, no one else exists –
my heart's now set to resist forced entry
from any other female entity
trying to break in to commit larceny
and steal my emotions.

Seduction

I pledge to stand – gallant Knight
defending lady's honour, the cause of right –
ready to fight to cast off demonic depression
with holy kiss
Change pained expression to angelic bliss.

I pledge to hold you, cherish you, make you feel safe
to let you know my heart is the safest place
for yours to rest – I'm uniquely blessed
to be a Lion with my own Lioness
to be allowed into the courts of an Empress
and yes....

I pledge my heart, my mind, my soul, my flesh
as two become one, as souls link and mesh.

Epilogue
Inspired

I'm Passionate -
I resonate
With expressions of rapture
As I capture the nuances of every breath
Held
And expelled
Whispering winds brought to silence
At the beauty of a red tinged sunset
The Earth paused
Awed
As winking sun bows low
Ending sizzling performance with a flourish
Giving way to muted Moon's flight
Delicate and light
Cool white lace ribbons
Sequined glitter on dusky dress
Twirling gracefully before eager eyesight
And my hands are compelled to write
As dusk fades into brilliant night.

About the Author

Robert R. Gibson is called many things - from the 'Loovvveee Man' to the 'King of Hearts'- but his stage name accurately describes this master of seduction. As **PassionPoet**, he thrills audiences with powerful penetrative strokes of his pen; his words incite intense emotions in anyone who sees him perform or reads his poetry.

He has published his first book – EROTIC – in February 2014. This, his second book of erotic poetry, which is, for all intents and purposes, a sequel to EROTIC, was first published in 2015, and has now been republished as a second edition in 2023.

www.ingramcontent.com/pod-product-compliance
Lightning Source LLC
LaVergne TN
LVHW061554070526
838199LV00077B/7039